The Road To Myself

Where the heart learns to heal

Romasha Pandey

India | USA | UK

Copyright © Romasha Pandey
All Rights Reserved.

This book has been self-published with all reasonable efforts taken to make the material error-free by the author. No part of this book shall be used, reproduced in any manner whatsoever without written permission from the author, except in the case of brief quotations embodied in critical articles and reviews.

The Author of this book is solely responsible and liable for its content including but not limited to the views, representations, descriptions, statements, information, opinions, and references ["Content"]. The Content of this book shall not constitute or be construed or deemed to reflect the opinion or expression of the Publisher or Editor. Neither the Publisher nor Editor endorse or approve the Content of this book or guarantee the reliability, accuracy, or completeness of the Content published herein and do not make any representations or warranties of any kind, express or implied, including but not limited to the implied warranties of merchantability, fitness for a particular purpose.

The Publisher and Editor shall not be liable whatsoever...

Made with ❤ on the BookLeaf Publishing Platform
www.bookleafpub.in
www.bookleafpub.com

Dedication

For the memory of my cat, whose quiet presence inspired me;
for coffee, which keeps my ideas awake;
and for my overthinking brain, which somehow wrote all of this anyway;
and for my teacher who believed in my words long before I did.

Preface

Dear Reader,

These poems are my whispered conversations with the world, emotions I couldn't always speak aloud, thoughts that only paper could hold. A wise person once said that paper has more patience than people, and I have found that to be true. Joy, sorrow, hope, and reflection drift across the lines. Each one is a fragment of my heart made visible.

My companions on this journey were many: the gentle memory of my cat, whose quiet presence inspired me, the steady warmth of coffee that kept ideas awake, and my overthinking brain, which never ceases to wander and wonder. Together they coaxed my thoughts into words, transforming fleeting feelings into poems.

As you turn these pages, I hope you sense the pulse behind them, the small sparks of laughter, the quiet sighs of memory, the moments that linger in the corners of life. Perhaps you will see pieces of your own story reflected here, or simply pause to witness mine.

Thank you for walking into this world with me, for letting these poems breathe, and for sharing in the delicate, messy, beautiful act of expression.

Acknowledgements

This book wouldn't exist without the people who became my light when words felt heavy.

To Miss Divya — thank you for believing in me when I didn't believe in myself. Your kindness, patience, and understanding shaped not just my writing, but the person I am becoming. You helped me give voice to thoughts I once kept silent and guided me through every stumble with warmth and strength. Her encouragement turned hesitation into courage, and her belief in my writing has left a mark on every page of this book.

To the memory of my cat, whose silent presence inspired many lines and whose spirit lingers in every quiet corner of these pages.

To my notebook, faithful companion and keeper of thoughts, for never judging, always listening, and holding every stray idea until it became a poem.

And finally, to you, the reader, for stepping into this little world of words, where emotions, memories, and imagination wander freely.

I. Fractured sunlight

There are days when breathing feels like lifting mountains,
when every heartbeat echoes too loudly,
and the mirror holds a stranger's reflection,
eyes heavy with questions the world won't answer.
I have stood in the silence between courage and collapse,
where the smallest step forward burns like fire,
and even light feels too bright to touch.
In those moments, I learned the shape of strength,
not loud, not shining,
but trembling, quiet,
still refusing to fall.
The sky does not always open with mercy.
Sometimes, it rains until it forgets how to stop,
and I stand beneath it, drenched in all the versions of me that didn't make it here.
But struggle, I've learned, is a secret sculptor.
It carves us with its blunt hands,
shaping what we are meant to become.
So even in the ache, even in the chaos,
I whisper to myself:
This is not the end,
this is how strength is born.
In the depths of shadow, I find a flicker,

a spark of resilience igniting the dark,
and step by step, I weave a tapestry
of every moment that dared to break me.
With each thread pulled tight, I rise anew,
an unfinished song with verses unspoken,
proclaiming that beauty can thrive in the wreckage,
and from the ashes, a fire still awakens.

II. Veil of questions

Doubt does not arrive like thunder.
It slips in quietly,
Through the cracks of a thought,
the pause before a decision,
the glance at someone who seems more certain than me.
It whispers in the spaces where I used to trust myself,
asks questions I can't answer,
plants roots in the soil of my hesitation.
And soon, every choice feels like walking through fog,
every step forward
a step away from clarity.
I have stared at blank pages
and wondered if my words meant anything.
I have looked at my dreams
and thought they looked better in someone else's hands.
But doubt, I've realized,
is not an enemy,
it's a mirror.
It shows me what I fear losing,
what I care about enough to question.
And sometimes, when I breathe through it long enough,
the fog thins,
and I see that the path was never gone,
only hidden until I was brave enough

to walk through the mist.
Yet here I stand,
with the weight of my own reflections,
not as a prisoner of uncertainty,
but as a traveler seeking light,
and in the tremor of each step,
I find strength in fragility,
an echo of resilience rising from the depths.
For in the quietude, where doubt dared to linger,
I discover the flicker of possibility,
the gentle reminder that even clouds
must part to let the sun break through.

III. Flame in the fog

Fear wears many faces.
Sometimes it's the tremor in my voice
when I have something true to say.
Sometimes it's silence,
a silence so heavy
it drowns the sound of courage.
It hides in the corners of my mind,
where I store all the "what ifs,"
each one a ghost that refuses to leave.
What if I fail?
What if I'm not enough?
What if the world laughs at the sound of my becoming?
But one day,
I stopped running from it.
I turned around
and looked fear in the eye.
It wasn't a monster.
It was a reflection,
a younger me, trembling,
begging to be understood.
So, I reached out,
held its shaking hand,
and walked forward anyway.
Because bravery was never the absence of fear,

it was learning to dance
with the very thing that tried to stop me.

IV. Rivers that forget

At first, I held it close.
Anger,
warm, sharp, alive.
It felt like protection,
like a fire I could control
when everything else burned without reason.
I carried it in my chest,
fed it with every memory that stung,
every word that cut too deep to forget.
It made me strong, I thought.
but strength built on bitterness
cracks when touched by kindness.
One night, I watched the stars
and realized how quiet they were.
No fury, no flames, just light
that refused to go out.
And I wondered,
what if I could glow like that,
not burn?
So, I let the fire fade.
It didn't vanish all at once,
it sighed, flickered, softened.
And in its ashes, I found something
I had buried long ago:

peace.
Anger had built walls around me,
but forgiveness, it built doors.
And when I stepped through,
the air felt new,
like the first breath after rain.
I tasted hope,
a sweetness that lingered,
a whisper of blooms unfurling,
soft petals brushing against my heart.
I learned to dance with shadows,
to weave my past into light,
not as a burden,
but as a thread in the tapestry of tomorrow.

V. Wind through the windows

Change doesn't knock politely.
It walks in, rearranges the furniture of your life,
and leaves the door open.
Suddenly, the things that once fit
feel too small to hold you.
I used to cling,
to voices, to faces,
to days that smelled like certainty.
I thought letting go meant losing,
but maybe it's just another word for growing.
Seasons don't ask the trees
if they're ready to shed their leaves.
The trees simply trust
that spring will return.
So I am learning to trust too.
To watch the old fall away
without mourning it too long.
To let unfamiliar mornings unfold
without rushing to label them "different."
Maybe change is not a thief,
maybe it's a quiet teacher,
reminding me that even endings
can feel like beginnings

when met with an open heart.
And in those tender moments,
when fear whispers of the past,
I'll breathe deep, embrace the unknown,
and dance with the shadows of tomorrow,
knowing each step, though uncertain,
writes a new story in the dust of today.

VI. Petals in the rain

Healing never arrived as thunder.
It tiptoed in,
with morning light spilling through curtains,
with the hum of a song I'd forgotten I loved.
It hid in the smallest things,
the first sip of coffee,
the soft stretch of a lazy cat,
the pages of a book that smelled like yesterday.
The world didn't change,
I just began noticing the parts
that stayed kind when everything else didn't.
Some days, joy was a single blooming flower,
or the quiet of rain against my window.
Other days, it was simply
the courage to get out of bed.
I used to chase healing
like a finish line,
but now I know,
it lives in moments
too small to measure,
too gentle to grasp.
They gather slowly,
like drops forming a river,
until one day you realize,

you are no longer drowning.
You are flowing.

VII. Hands that held

When the world grew heavy,
I thought I had to carry it alone.
My hands trembled under the weight
of everything unsaid,
and silence began to sound like surrender.
Then,
someone reached out.
Not to lift it all,
but to remind me that I didn't have to.
Sometimes it was a word,
sometimes just presence,
the kind that said,
"I'm here,"
without asking for anything in return.
It wasn't always grand,
support rarely is.
It's in the shared laugh
that cracks open a tired heart,
the message that arrives
when you've forgotten you still matter.
People don't always fix your pain.
But they hold it gently,
so you can breathe again.
And maybe that's what love really means,

not saving someone from their storms,
but sitting beside them
until the clouds pass on their own.
In those moments,
the shadows lightened,
and I learned to share the burden,
to let hope weave through the cracks,
finding strength in the soft glow
of a hand that wouldn't let go.
Together, we weather the tempests,
each gust a reminder—
I am not alone in this journey,
the world, still heavy,
but lighter somehow
when heart meets heart.

VIII. Lanterns of the past

Memories are teachers
who never ask to be thanked.
They linger quietly,
in photographs, in scents,
in songs that ache with recognition.
Some arrive wrapped in laughter,
others sting before they soothe.
But every one of them
leaves a trace,
a whisper
of who I used to be,
and who I'm still becoming.
I've learned that not all memories
are meant to be held too tightly.
Some are lessons wearing familiar faces,
reminding me that even the hurt
had purpose.
The moments I thought would break me
taught me patience.
The ones I took for granted
taught me gratitude.
And the ones I miss the most
taught me how to cherish what remains.
Maybe that's what growing up is,

learning to thank the past
for all its bruises and brilliance,
and walking forward
a little wiser,
a little softer.

IX. Whispering leaves

There are days when the noise in my head
feels louder than the world outside.
On those days, I go where silence still lives,
where the trees don't rush to speak,
and the wind hums softly,
as though it knows the weight I'm carrying.
The earth has a language of its own,
and if you listen closely enough,
you begin to understand it.
The rustle of leaves sounds like forgiveness.
The waves against the shore whisper,
begin again.
The rain doesn't apologize for falling,
it simply does, and the world is cleaner for it.
I've watched sunlight weave its way
through cracks in old bark,
reminding me that beauty doesn't fear imperfection.
I've seen flowers bloom in forgotten corners,
teaching me that hope often grows
where no one thought to look.
When I sit beneath a tree,
I imagine its roots,
deep, patient, unhurried.
It doesn't compare its pace

to the one beside it.
It grows when it's ready,
and rests when it must.
I think maybe healing is like that too.
Nature never demands that I explain myself.
It doesn't ask me to be better,
only to *be.*
To breathe.
To remember that I am a small,
but necessary part
of something infinite.
And when I leave,
with dust on my shoes
and a lighter heart in my chest,
I realize that the world didn't fix me.
It just reminded me how to listen
to the quiet places inside myself.

X. Mirror lake

There are evenings when I sit by the window,
and the world outside feels far too vast,
too filled with noise and names
and all the versions of me I've tried to become.
In the glass, my reflection looks back,
familiar, yet changed.
Not the same girl who once believed
every silence was an ending,
every mistake a flaw carved in stone.
I stare at her,
and she stares back,
as if asking me to remember
that growing is not the same as losing.
That I am allowed to outgrow the hands
I once held tightly,
the fears I once named "home."
Reflection is not always gentle.
It brings back faces, choices,
moments I'd rather forget.
But it also brings light,
the kind that falls softly through leaves,
revealing the dust motes of my becoming.
I've learned that to look inward
is not to drown,

it's to dive deep enough
to see what still glows beneath the surface.
And sometimes,
that glow is faint, trembling,
but it's there.
So I write, I pause, I breathe.
I trace the outlines of who I was
and who I might still be.
And in that quiet space between the two,
I whisper a promise to myself,
to be patient with the process,
to be kind to the mirror,
and to love even the versions of me
that are still learning how to begin.

XI. Dawn within

It comes quietly,
not as thunder,
but as a soft flicker of understanding
in the dim corners of thought.
Insight doesn't shout,
it listens first.
It waits beneath confusion,
beneath the noise of certainty,
and then, when you've stopped looking for it,
it breathes.
I used to think wisdom was loud,
a declaration, a moment of clarity
you could frame in words.
But it's gentler than that.
It's the pause before you speak.
It's realizing that not every question
deserves an answer right away.
Sometimes, insight arrives disguised as pain,
a lesson wrapped in ache.
It asks you to sit with what hurts,
to see beyond it,
to find the message hidden
between what was lost
and what was learned.

Other times, it comes as peace,
the kind you don't notice until later,
when your heart no longer races
at the thought of what could've been.
I think insight is like light filtered through trees,
never blinding, always shifting.
It doesn't change the forest,
but it helps you see it differently.
And maybe that's all we ever need,
not to know everything,
but to understand just enough
to move forward
with gentler eyes,
and a steadier heart.

XII. Golden threads

There are mornings when the world feels gentle
the air still,
as if holding its breath before a beginning.
In those moments, I see it,
a golden thread,
thin as sunlight spilling through curtains,
weaving through everything I've ever loved.
It shimmers through the hands that once held mine,
through the laughter caught between cups of coffee,
through my mother's voice,
soft as the hum of an old lullaby
that still lingers in the corners of my mind.
It runs through the letters I never sent,
and the tears I quietly let fall,
for every person I met
who unknowingly stitched a piece of themselves
into the fabric of my becoming.
Gratitude is not loud.
It doesn't arrive with fanfare or fireworks.
It whispers.
It hides in the pauses between heartbeats,
in the gentle rhythm of breathing,
in the small act of waking up again
after the world felt too heavy to face.

It's in the rain tapping softly on the window,
reminding me that life still moves,
that even clouds need to empty themselves
to feel light again.
It's in the books I've marked with trembling fingers,
where I once underlined a sentence
that seemed to understand me
better than I understood myself.
There was a time I mistook gratitude
for grand gestures,
thank-you speeches, gifts wrapped in silver paper.
But now I see it clearer.
It's the quiet thing that lives beneath everything else,
holding the fragile edges of the world together.
It's the reason we keep going,
even when the map fades
and the road bends into uncertainty.
When I look back,
I realize that I have been guided all along,
by hands I could not see,
by moments that could have easily gone unnoticed.
A teacher who saw something in me
before I dared to see it myself.
A friend who stayed
when silence was the only language I could speak.
A memory that still aches,
but somehow glows softer with each passing year.

Gratitude isn't the absence of pain.
It is its quiet companion,
the hand that steadies the trembling heart,
the light that filters through grief
and turns it into something bearable.
I think we're all stitched together
by this invisible thread,
every act of kindness,
every lesson carved from loss,
every breath that becomes a promise
to keep living, even when it hurts.
And maybe that's all we ever need to do:
to follow the thread,
to trace it back to the people, the places,
the small mercies that remind us
that even in our loneliest hours,
we are part of something vast,
something golden,
something that holds.

XIII. The hidden garden

There was a time I forgot
how to listen to myself.
The noise of the world grew too loud
everyone speaking in shoulds and musts,
until my own voice
became a whisper buried beneath their echoes.
Days passed like strangers.
I wore smiles that didn't belong to me,
spoke words that tasted unfamiliar,
and mistook survival
for living.
But healing doesn't begin with thunder.
it begins quietly
with a hand reaching toward the soil,
with the courage to plant something small
in a place long abandoned.
One day, I returned
to the corners of my heart I had once closed.
There was dust on the windows,
silence heavy on the air,
and yet, beneath the stillness,
I could hear something breathing.
Faintly. Patiently.
Like the first stirrings of spring

beneath a stubborn winter.
I knelt beside my own weariness,
and there it was
a hidden garden,
wild, untrimmed,
but alive.
The roots were tangled with old regrets,
the flowers bent under the weight of forgotten dreams.
Yet when I touched them,
they leaned toward the light
as if they still remembered
how to grow.
In that moment,
I understood that rediscovery
is not about becoming someone new.
It's about returning
to the person you left behind
when the world told you to be smaller.
It's finding the laughter
you once buried under expectations,
the softness you replaced with armor,
the spark you called naïve
but was only ever human.
Now, I water this garden
with gentleness instead of guilt.
I let the rain of forgiveness
wash the dirt from my hands.

I let the sun touch
even the parts of me
I once hid in shadow.
Every day, something blooms,
a piece of courage,
a whisper of peace,
a forgotten dream stretching its arms again.
And though weeds still grow,
I do not rush to pluck them,
even imperfection
has its place in this soil.
The hidden garden within me
is no longer silent.
It hums with second chances,
with the scent of self-acceptance,
with the quiet music
of roots learning to hold again.
And perhaps this is what it means
to find yourself again,
not to be unbroken,
but to grow beautifully around the cracks.

XIV. Glow in the dark

Compassion is not loud.
It does not demand attention
or parade its presence.
It moves softly, like sunlight
through a cracked window,
falling where it is needed
without asking for permission.
It is the hand that lifts another
when the weight of the world
is too heavy to carry alone.
The hand that does not judge
but offers warmth
where there was only cold.
I have seen it in quiet gestures:
a friend who listens
without interrupting,
a stranger who offers a smile
in a moment too dark to see hope,
a hand extended
without expectation,
without notice,
yet changing everything.
Compassion is patient.
It bends to the curve of another's sorrow,

reaches into the hollow places
we hide from even ourselves,
and gently reminds us
that we are not alone.
Sometimes, it comes to me
like a spark through my own hands,
a chance to heal someone else
and, in doing so,
to heal a piece of myself.
It does not erase pain,
but it lights it,
illuminates the edges,
so we may see
what is broken,
what is growing,
and what deserves care.
Hands of light are everywhere,
woven into the small acts we often overlook.
The words we speak,
the patience we offer,
the forgiveness we give
all threads of illumination
that make the dark corners of life
a little less frightening,
a little more human.
To practice compassion
is to hold space for another soul

and, in that act,
to find the light in your own.

XV. Rising saplings

Growth is not sudden.
It does not announce itself with fireworks
or the clamor of triumph.
It creeps quietly,
like green shoots through cracked earth,
like saplings reaching for sunlight
in a garden left untended.
I have been one of those saplings,
fragile, uncertain, bending
under winds I could not control.
My roots tangled with doubt,
my leaves trembling in storms
I could not shelter from.
But day by day,
I learned to stretch a little farther,
to push past the shadows
that made me believe
I was smaller than I truly was.
Growth is in the patient persistence,
the slow turning of the seasons,
the way the earth softens
even after being trampled.
I discovered that growth is not perfection.
It is the courage to survive the frost,

to heal the wounds left by past storms,
to let the rain fall and trust
that it will nourish, not destroy.
Every choice,
every mistake,
every tender act
adds a ring to my trunk,
a layer of strength I can carry forward.
Growth does not erase the scars,
but it teaches me to bend, not break.
And so I rise,
like saplings stretching toward the sky,
each leaf a promise,
each branch a quiet testament
to patience, to resilience,
to the subtle power of time.
The garden I tend within myself
is wild, imperfect, alive.
And in its growth, I find
not just the courage to survive,
but the wonder of becoming
something taller, stronger,
and beautifully my own.

XVI. Paper boats

Letting go is not a single act.
It is a slow exhale,
a quiet folding of fragile paper
into boats meant to carry what we cannot keep.
I have held too tightly,
words I could not forget,
grudges I mistook for shields,
hopes that bent beneath the weight of reality.
They clung to me like vines,
tangled, sharp, and heavy.
But one day, I realized
these boats do not define me.
They are vessels, not anchors,
floating gently on the river of life.
And so I place them on the water,
watching them drift away,
light as feathers,
carrying the sorrow, the fear, the doubt
I no longer need to hold.
Letting go is learning that absence
does not erase love,
and that endings
can be beginnings
in disguise.

It is the courage to release
what no longer nourishes,
to trust the current
to guide it toward somewhere it belongs.
I watch the paper boats sail,
and I am left with space,
space to grow,
space to feel,
space to breathe.
Letting go is not forgetting.
It is remembering with tenderness,
without clinging too tightly.
It is the hand that unclenches,
the heart that opens,
the soul that trusts it can float
even after storms have passed.
And in that quiet liberation,
I discover something precious:
freedom is not taking everything with you.
Freedom is placing what must leave
into the river,
and watching it sail,
as you rise,
like a bird finally learning to fly.

XVII. Stars beyond the clouds

Hope is not always a blaze.
Sometimes it is a quiet light,
hidden beyond the weight of gray,
beyond the storms that stretch across the sky.
I have looked up and seen only clouds,
heavy, unyielding,
as if the world had swallowed every promise.
And yet, even then,
there is something waiting
a glimmer, a flicker,
soft and patient,
like stars beyond the clouds.
Hope is the courage to lift your eyes,
to trust that darkness
cannot last forever,
that light always finds a way
through the cracks.
It is the memory of laughter
when you thought you had forgotten how to smile,
the whisper of dreams
that refuse to die
even when fear has spoken louder.
Stars beyond the clouds are quiet teachers:

they remind me that
even when I cannot see the path,
it still exists.
Even when despair presses down,
something luminous endures.
Hope is patient.
It grows slowly,
a seed beneath frozen soil,
a warmth beneath winter's frost.
It does not shout,
but when it comes,
it changes everything,
softening hearts,
illuminating roads,
allowing life to rise again
after long nights.
And so I look up,
and even when clouds linger,
I know they cannot hide the stars forever.
Hope endures,
quiet and steady,
waiting to guide me
beyond the gray
to a sky I have yet to fully see.

XVIII. Skyward wings

Dreams are not always loud.
They do not arrive with applause
or the sparkle of immediate success.
Sometimes they are whispers,
faint as the wind brushing a forgotten path,
calling you forward
when every step feels uncertain.
I have hesitated,
held back by shadows of doubt,
by the voices that said I could not,
that whispered *stay small, stay safe.*
But dreams do not wait.
They stretch beyond fear,
beyond hesitation,
beyond the walls we build around ourselves.
To pursue them is to run
into the wind,
to climb even when the summit hides behind clouds,
to keep reaching
when the horizon seems farther
than any eyes can see.
Dreams are patient teachers.
They ask for courage,
for resilience,

for a heart willing to leap
even when certainty is absent.
They demand faith in the unseen,
trust in the impossible.
Each step I take toward them
is a spark,
a small rebellion against limits,
a quiet promise to myself
that I will not shrink,
that I will rise,
even if slowly,
even if stumbles come.
Skyward wings are not about arriving.
They are about daring.
About discovering strength
you didn't know was yours,
about painting your own sky
even when clouds obscure the sun.
And in the pursuit,
I find not only the dream,
but the courage,
the fire,
the self
I had been waiting to meet all along.

XIX. Hidden wellspring

Strength is not always visible.
It does not roar from mountaintops,
nor blaze like lightning across the sky.
Sometimes it glows quietly,
like embers beneath ash,
waiting for a breath of courage
to ignite them into fire.
I have searched for it in others,
in guidance, in applause,
in the assurance of someone saying,
"You can."
But true strength is something quieter,
something that rises from within,
from the deepest corners of a trembling heart.
It is in the moments you feel most small,
when fear presses heavy against your chest,
and yet you take a step anyway.
It is in the whispered promise
that you will continue,
even when the path bends
and the horizon seems lost.
Strength lives in patience,
in persistence,
in the courage to stand

even after falling.
It is found in the silence between breaths,
in the choice to keep moving,
to keep believing,
to keep showing up for yourself
when no one else can.
I learned that it is not flawless,
it is marred, imperfect,
but resilient.
Each scar, each struggle,
each tear shed and lesson learned
adds to its quiet brilliance,
like embers fanned into flame.
And when I finally notice it,
I see that it has always been there,
waiting,
humming beneath doubt,
ready to carry me
through storms, through shadows,
toward the light I had long forgotten
I could reach.
Strength is not taking on the world at once.
It is finding the ember within yourself
and letting it burn, steadily,
so that even in darkness,
even in uncertainty,
you rise,

bright and unbroken,
your own source of light.

XX. Sun on dew

Victories are not always loud.
They do not always come draped in banners,
nor crowned with applause.
Sometimes, they are petals
small, fragile,
but radiant enough
to make the heart swell.
I have overlooked them,
the quiet moments when I tried
and did not fail,
when I stood after stumbling,
when I smiled
even though the world felt heavy.
They seemed too small,
too insignificant,
yet they carried a light
that no one else could see.
Celebrating them is an art,
a practice of noticing.
It is in the first sip of warmth
after a long, cold morning,
the page finished in a journal
that had waited weeks for ink,
the tiny "yes" whispered to myself

when doubt knocked again.
These victories, though small,
are the roots of courage.
Each one strengthens the heart,
each one teaches patience,
each one reminds me
that growth is not always dramatic
but constant, persistent,
like petals unfolding toward the sun.
I gather them gently,
lining them like stepping stones
along the path I walk.
And when the world seems too loud,
too chaotic,
I remember that even the smallest triumphs
can guide me forward,
illuminating the journey
one quiet, shining step at a time.
Celebration is not always public.
It is a soft acknowledgment,
a nod to yourself,
a whispered gratitude
for simply showing up,
for trying,
for being here.
In this gentle recognition,
I find strength,

hope, and the courage to rise again,
to face the world
with petals of triumph
carried in my hands,
and the knowledge
that every small victory
is a step toward something greater.

XXI. Sealed letters

Closure is not a sudden door closing,
nor a loud declaration
that everything is finished.
It is the quiet folding of moments,
the gentle placing of memories
into a box lined with understanding,
where they can rest without pain.
I have carried echoes,
voices that lingered too long,
words I could not unsay,
dreams that bent beneath the weight of endings.
They circled my mind like restless birds,
never still, never quiet.
But closure comes softly,
like twilight after a long, restless day.
It whispers that what has passed
does not need to be carried anymore,
that letting go does not erase,
but transforms.
It is the courage to forgive,
even when the wound still stings,
the patience to release what cannot stay,
and the trust that life
will continue to offer new beginnings.

Closure lives in small gestures:
the last page of a journal turned,
the final note read aloud,
the quiet nod to a memory
that once hurt
but now teaches.
It is not forgetting.
It is remembering without pain,
holding without grasping,
learning to walk forward
with the past as a companion,
not a chain.
And when I finally feel it,
I sense a gentle unburdening,
a soft exhale from the corners of my heart,
and in that space,
I find room to breathe,
to grow,
to begin again.
Closure is not an ending.
It is the bridge between what was
and what can be,
a quiet promise
that life, with all its turns and fades,
still moves toward light.

XXII. The warmth of spring

No fanfare,
just the quiet hush of the thawing earth,
and the first chorus breaking through silence.
The wind that no longer bites, rather sings,
carrying the scent of something new, something soft.

The birdsong returns like forgotten verses, fluttering as it reaches our ears,
between branches dressed in light.
Puddles reflect a bluer sky, clouds drifting
like lazy thoughts and the sun, no longer sky.

Each breeze brushes against the skin, like a story I once knew,
one about hope,
wrapped in the scent of Jasmine and rain.

Spring doesn't ask you to be ready.
It simply arrives.
Arms open,
heart full,
and waits for you to bloom too.

XXIII. A ray of sunlight

She isn't a girl,
but a dawn unbuttoning the sky,
a golden hymn that slips
between the cracks of silence.
Her smile is the hush of petals opening,
a sudden blaze
that teaches shadows how to bow.
When she laughs,
the earth forgets its heaviness,
and trees stretch taller,
As if to drink her sound.
She walks,
and the pavements glimmer with a light of hope.
Her footsteps are echoes of summers,
reminding us that even in the darkest of places,
warmth still lies.
She holds the sun in her chest,
it doesn't burn
rather glows.
It is a steady flame that spills,
into every pair of weary pair of hands
that dare to come her way.
Grief dissolves against her presence,
like frost breaking under dawn.

Even silence is altered,
becoming music,
so melodious, they could be mistaken for Mozart's.
Her eyes,
appear as two small constellations,
where the universe hides,
its softest secrets.
Gazing into them feels ethereal,
like learning a new language of light
once known as a child
but forgotten over time.
She, is the reason windows open,
the reason wind carries fragrances,
the reason a field of wildflower
believes in itself.
Joy doesn't describe her.
She is joy,
woven into flesh,
draped in mortality,
but never entirely earthbound
because her shine scatters across galaxies.
Perhaps that is why
when she leaves,
her absence still glows,
on the walls of memory
like sunlight that lingers,
long after dusk has claimed the sky.

And in that twilight's embrace,
we find her laughter woven in shadows,
a reminder that love refuses to fade,
it dances in the corners of our dreams,
etching warmth into the coldest nights,
until the dawn beckons once more,
and she returns,
with wings stitched from the fabric of light.

www.ingramcontent.com/pod-product-compliance
Lightning Source LLC
Chambersburg PA
CBHW070458050426
42449CB00012B/3022